Chocolate Animals

Frances McNaughton

Search Press

First published in Great Britain 2012

Search Press Limited
Wellwood, North Farm Road,
Tunbridge Wells, Kent TN2 3DR

Text copyright © Frances McNaughton 2012

Photographs by Debbie Patterson at
Search Press Studios

Photographs and design copyright
© Search Press Ltd 2012

ISBN: 978-1-84448-845-2

Suppliers
If you have difficulty in obtaining any of the
materials and equipment mentioned in this
book, then please visit the Search Press website
for details of suppliers: www.searchpress.com

Printed in Malaysia

Contents

Introduction 4

Basic shapes 6

Tools and materials 7

Mouse 8

Baby Seal 10

Quick Bunny 12

Baby Gorilla 14

Chipmunk 16

Kitten 18

Badger 20

Poodle 22

Mole 24

Guinea Pig 26

Giraffe 28

Porcupine 30

Armadillo 32

Goat 34

Sleeping Bear 36

Otter 38

Leopard Gecko 40

Pony 42

Reindeer 44

Prairie Dog 46

Introduction

Modelling chocolate is lovely to work with and tastes great. It is versatile as it holds its shape well and models can be worked on over a few hours. It can be used for sculpture, in moulds, for making roses and other flowers, bows and fans, and even for covering cakes. It can be rolled very thinly and cut for fur and hair effects. Fingerprints and unwanted marks can be polished out by gently rubbing over the surface with your fingers. It blends into itself easily to achieve a beautifully smooth finish. No 'glue' is needed to stick pieces together – pressing firmly with fingers or the Dresden tool should be enough (occasionally it may be helpful to warm the tool in hot water before pressing two pieces together).

There are a number of different commercial chocolate modelling pastes available in sugarcraft and cake decorating shops, but it is easy to make at home. Any chocolate without fillings and additions is suitable, so you can use your favourite, or normal cooking chocolate. For the models in this book I used white, milk and dark chocolate without adding any colouring (apart from a little black for the eyes). All the different shades were made by mixing the different pastes together. If coloured models are desired, the chocolate modelling paste can be made with coloured candy melts, or using white chocolate with the addition of powdered colours or non-water-based colours suitable for chocolate.

The animals made in this book could also be made in other edible and non-edible modelling pastes. For more modelling ideas, check out my other books in this series, particularly *Sugar Animals* and *Sugar Birds,* which have creatures which could be adapted to be made in chocolate modelling paste.

Recipe for white, milk or dark chocolate modelling paste

Use half the weight of gently warmed liquid glucose to melted chocolate, e.g. 100g (3½oz) chocolate: 50g (1¾oz) liquid glucose. The advantage of working with proportions in weight is that it is very easy to adapt to smaller or larger amounts.

Melt the chocolate in a bowl set over a pan of simmering water. Leave to cool for a few minutes. Heat the liquid glucose gently in a separate bowl set over the pan of simmering water. Gradually mix the chocolate into the glucose, making a thick paste that leaves the sides of the bowl clean. Place in a plastic bag and leave for about an hour until set.

The modelling paste can be used as it is, but you may find it easier to handle if mixed with a little sugarpaste (cake covering/ rolled fondant). I used the ratio 2 parts chocolate modelling paste: 1 part sugarpaste. This keeps the lovely chocolate flavour.

In warm environments it may be necessary to cool the paste in a fridge for a short time to keep it workable.

In the US many people use light corn syrup instead of liquid glucose to make chocolate modelling paste. Use half the weight of the light corn syrup to the melted chocolate, as for liquid glucose above.

Chocolate modelling paste will keep for several months if wrapped well in plastic and kept airtight.

Basic shapes

Shapes

Chocolate modelling paste is best worked at room temperature. It is very firm to use when cold, and can become oily when you handle it if it is too warm, so I have kept the models in this book reasonably small to make them easier to handle. The sizes could all be adapted to make larger or smaller models if required. To avoid problems of over-handling, place shaped pieces on a workboard when adding details.

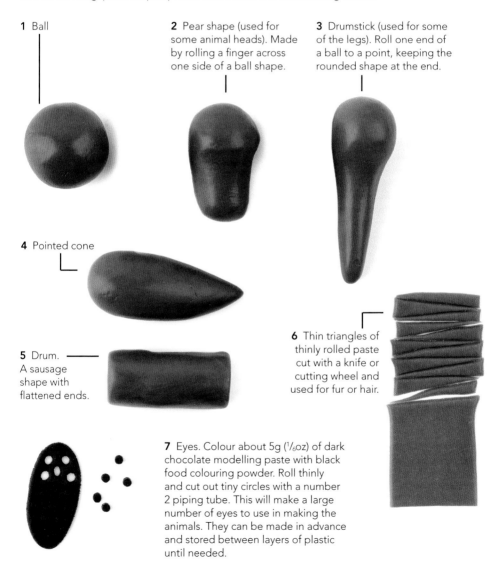

1 Ball

2 Pear shape (used for some animal heads). Made by rolling a finger across one side of a ball shape.

3 Drumstick (used for some of the legs). Roll one end of a ball to a point, keeping the rounded shape at the end.

4 Pointed cone

5 Drum. A sausage shape with flattened ends.

6 Thin triangles of thinly rolled paste cut with a knife or cutting wheel and used for fur or hair.

7 Eyes. Colour about 5g (¹⁄₆oz) of dark chocolate modelling paste with black food colouring powder. Roll thinly and cut out tiny circles with a number 2 piping tube. This will make a large number of eyes to use in making the animals. They can be made in advance and stored between layers of plastic until needed.

Tools and materials

Liquid glucose

Texturing sponge (a clean, unused scouring pad)

Small sharp pointed scissors

5cm (2in) oval cutter

Small sieve/tea strainer

Heart cutters

Chocolate

Number 2 plain piping tube

Inexpensive digital jewellery scales (available on the internet)

Drinking straw cut at an angle for the mouth shape

Fine paintbrush

Small fine palette knife

Dogbone/ball tool

Smile tool (petal veiner tool)

Dresden tool

Cutting wheel

Waterbrush filled with alcohol or lemon essence for painting

Non-stick rolling pin

Icing sugar and cocoa powder for finishing touches

Clear uncoloured piping gel (also available in pots which could be put into a piping bag fitted with a fine piping tube). Piping gel is optional – it gives the eyes a pleasing shine.

Mouse

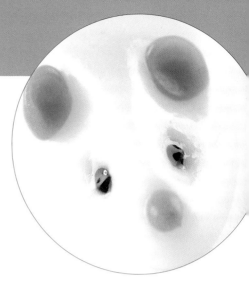

Materials:

10g (⅓oz) white chocolate modelling paste

Edible black eyes (see page 6)

5g (⅙oz) of pale chocolate modelling paste (mix milk chocolate with white chocolate), for nose, ears and tail

Piping gel

Tools:

Small palette knife

Dresden tool

Dogbone/ball tool

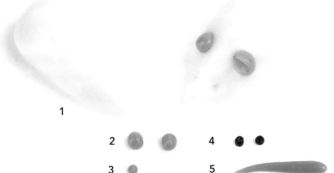

Instructions:

1 Shape the white chocolate modelling paste to a 4cm (1½in) long cone. Pinch gently at the head end.

2 Indent for the nose and eyes with the Dresden tool. Make two very small balls (0.5cm/¼in) of pale chocolate modelling paste for the ears. Lay them in position and push them in with the small end of the dogbone/ball tool, supporting the back of the ear with your finger to help to cup it.

3 Attach a very tiny ball of pale chocolate modelling paste for the nose.

4 Push the black eyes in with the Dresden tool.

5 For the tail, roll a 0.5cm (¼in) ball of pale chocolate modelling paste into a 3cm (1¼in) carrot shape. Attach the thick end to the tail end of the body, then loop it up and over the back.

6 Squeeze a little piping gel into the eyes to make them look rounded and shiny.

Baby Seal

Materials:

10g (1/3oz) white chocolate modelling paste

Edible black eyes (see page 6)

Tiny ball of dark chocolate modelling paste for nose

Piping gel

Icing sugar

Tools:

Small palette knife

Dresden tool

Smile tool/drinking straw

Small sieve

Instructions:

1 Make two front paws by rolling a tiny pea-sized (0.5cm) (¼in) piece of white chocolate modelling paste. Cut it in half. Press the paws with a finger to flatten them. Mark 'fingers' with a knife.

2 For the body, roll the rest of the paste to form a 5cm (2in) oval, pointed at one end and rounded at the other.

3 Cut 1cm (3/8in) into the pointed end with a knife and turn the cut edge under to make the tail. Press with a finger to flatten it. Mark the tail with a knife.

4 Mark cheeks/a mouth with the smile tool and indent for the nose, eyes and eyebrows with the Dresden tool.

5 Attach the front paws under the body.

6 For the nose, make a very tiny ball of dark chocolate modelling paste. Press it on to the face. Mark nostrils with a Dresden tool.

7 Press the black eyes in place, using the Dresden tool to push them in.

8 Sprinkle icing sugar over the seal using a small sieve to make it look soft and snowy (avoid getting icing sugar in his eyes).

9 Squeeze a little piping gel into the eyes to make them look rounded and shiny.

Quick Bunny

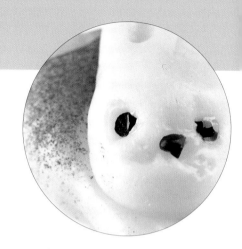

Materials:

10g (⅓oz) white chocolate modelling paste

Edible black eyes (see page 6)

Tiny ball of pale chocolate modelling paste (see Mouse, page 8)

Piping gel

Cocoa powder

Tools:

Small palette knife

Dresden tool

Dogbone/ball tool

Smile tool/drinking straw

Small sieve

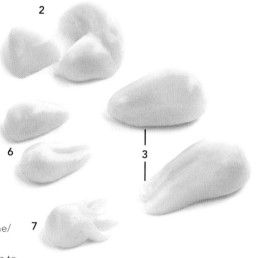

Instructions:

1 Make a tiny ball of white chocolate modelling paste for the tail.

2 Make a ball with the rest of the white chocolate modelling paste. Mark it into four. Cut one quarter for the head, the other three quarters will form the body.

3 Roll the body piece to a pointed 3cm (1¼in) cone. Cut 1cm (⅜in) into the pointed end with a knife and turn the cut edge under.

4 Mark toes with a knife. Indent with a dogbone/ball tool for the tail. Attach the tail.

5 Press in with your finger at the top of the legs to make a dip to hold the head.

6 Roll the head to a pointed 2cm (¾in) cone. Cut 1cm (⅜in) into the pointed end with a knife and turn the cut edge under.

7 Press the Dresden tool into the ears to shape them.

8 Attach the head at the top of the legs. Mark cheeks/a mouth with the smile tool. Indent for the nose and eyes with the Dresden tool.

9 Push black eyes in with Dresden tool. Make a tiny nose with pale chocolate modelling paste. Press into place.

10 Sprinkle cocoa powder over the bunny using a small sieve to make it look soft and furry (avoid getting cocoa in his eyes).

11 Squeeze a little piping gel into the eyes to make them look rounded and shiny.

Hop Chocolate

These bunnies are incredibly quick to make and once you get the hang of it, they will be multiplying like rabbits! The alternative is made with pale chocolate modelling paste with a white tail.

13

Baby Gorilla

Materials:

30g (1oz) dark chocolate modelling paste

Edible black eyes (see page 6)

5g (1/6oz) milk chocolate modelling paste

Piping gel

Tools:

Small palette knife

Non-stick rolling pin

Dresden tool

Dogbone/ball tool

Heart cutter, 1.25cm (½in)

2

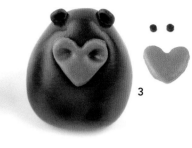

3

8

4

5

— 7 —

6

Instructions:

1 For the body, make a 2.5cm (1in) fat cone using 20g (²/₃oz) dark chocolate modelling paste.

2 For the ears, make two tiny balls of dark chocolate modelling paste. Lay the ears in position and push them in with the small end of the dogbone/ball tool, supporting the back of the ear with your finger to help to cup it to a rounded shape.

3 Use the non-stick rolling pin to roll out the milk chocolate modelling paste thinly. Cut out the heart shape. Press it on to the body. Indent for the eyes using the Dresden tool. Insert the black eyes.

4 Shape a tiny sausage of the milk chocolate paste and attach above the eyes for the forehead. Mark it with the Dresden tool to make wrinkles and a dip in the middle.

5 Make a small bean shape of the milk chocolate paste 1cm (³/₈in) long for the muzzle. Attach it to the face. Use a knife to mark a wide, smiling mouth.

6 Attach a tiny oval of dark chocolate modelling paste for the nose. Mark the nostrils with the Dresden tool.

7 For the hands and feet, cut a small pea-sized ball of milk chocolate modelling paste into four. Shape them all to form flat ovals. Mark them with a knife or Dresden tool to form fingers and thumbs; make two left-handed and two right-handed.

14

8 Cut a 10g (¹/₃oz) ball of dark chocolate modelling paste into four to make arms and legs. Roll each to a 2.5cm (1in) sausage and bend in the middle. Attach to the body. Press the hands and feet in place at the ends of the arms and legs.

9 Squeeze a little piping gel into the eyes to make them look rounded and shiny.

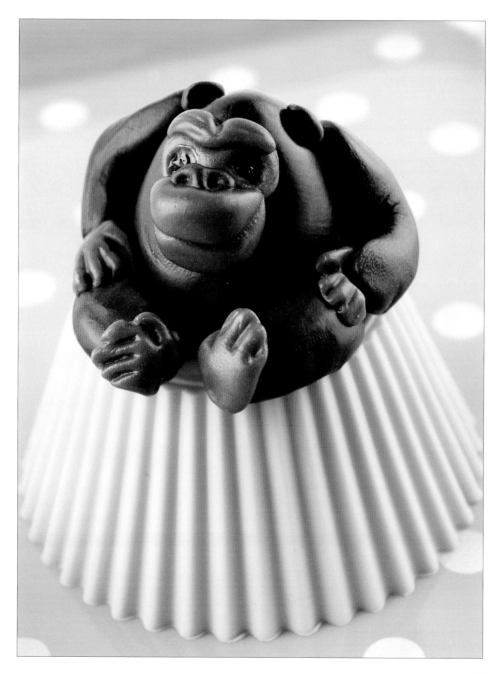

Chipmunk

Materials:

20g (²/₃oz) pale chocolate modelling paste: 20g (²/₃oz) white chocolate modelling paste mixed with a pinch of milk chocolate modelling paste

Edible black eyes (see page 6)

5g (¹/₆oz) white chocolate modelling paste

5g (¹/₆oz) milk chocolate modelling paste

Piping gel

Tools:

Small palette knife

Dresden tool

Instructions:

1 For the body, shape 10g (¹/₃oz) pale chocolate modelling paste to a 4cm (1½in) oval. Roll between your fingers to form a neck. Pinch the head forward to a point for the nose.

2 Make two tiny pieces of white chocolate modelling paste about the size of a rice grain. Press on to each side of the face. Indent for the eyes and ears using the Dresden tool. Insert black eyes.

3 Attach a tiny milk chocolate modelling paste triangle for the nose.

4 For the back legs, shape two 1g (0.04oz) balls of pale chocolate paste to 2cm (¾in) cones. Flatten the rounded end slightly and roll towards the foot. Mark toes with a knife. Attach to the body, pressing both on at the same time.

5 For the front legs, make two 0.5g (0.02oz) balls of paste to 1cm (³/₈in) carrot shapes. Mark toes with a knife. Attach to the body, pressing both on at the same time.

6 For the stripe and tail, shape 2g (0.1oz) of milk chocolate modelling paste to a 6cm (2³/₈in) pointed sausage, and 0.5g (0.02oz) of white chocolate modelling paste to a 5cm (2in) pointed sausage. Gently press the white sausage on top of the milk chocolate sausage, stroking to smooth them together. Attach from the top of the head and down the back, and forming the tail.

7 Squeeze a little piping gel into the eyes to make them look rounded and shiny.

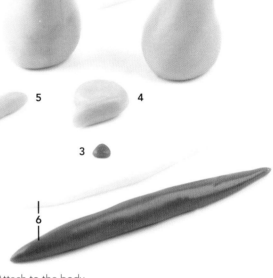

Kitten

Materials:

20g (²/₃oz) dark chocolate modelling paste

Edible black eyes (see page 6)

5g (¹/₆oz) white chocolate modelling paste

Tiny ball of pale chocolate modelling paste (see Mouse, page 8) for nose

Piping gel

Tools:

Small palette knife

Dresden tool

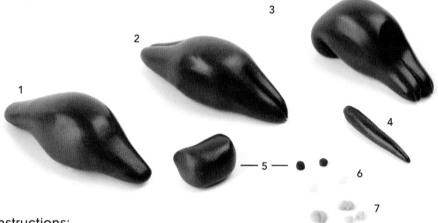

Instructions:

1 For the body, roll 10g (¹/₃oz) of the dark chocolate modelling paste to form a 5cm (2in) oval, pointed at each end.

2 Cut 1cm (³/₈in) into each pointed end with a knife and turn the cut edges under.

3 Bend the body so that the back legs go under the body and the front legs are outstretched. Mark toes for the front paws with a knife. Make an indentation at the top of the legs where the head will go.

4 For the tail, make a small pea of dark chocolate modelling paste. Roll it to a carrot shape 2.5cm (1in) long. Attach the fat end of the tail to the body, and curve the tail up.

5 For the head, shape a 2g (0.1oz) ball of dark chocolate modelling paste to a 1.5cm (⁵/₈in) oval. Pinch to form two ears. Indent the ears and eyes with the Dresden tool. Insert black eyes.

6 Make two tiny ovals of white chocolate modelling paste for the cheeks and press them on to the face.

7 For the nose, you need a tiny triangle, so make a tiny ball of pale chocolate modelling paste, and cut it into four segments. This will make four triangles, which is useful if you want to make more than one kitten. Press the nose into place.

8 Squeeze a little piping gel into the eyes to make them look rounded and shiny.

18

Playful Pair

The white kitten is made from white chocolate modelling paste with pale chocolate cheeks, and a dusting of cocoa powder. Cat lovers will pounce on a cake with these cute and tasty characters on top.

Badger

Materials:

10g (¹⁄₃oz) dark chocolate modelling paste

5g (¹⁄₆oz) white chocolate modelling paste

Edible black eyes (see page 6)

Tiny ball of pale chocolate modelling paste (see Mouse, page 8) for nose

Piping gel

Icing sugar

Tools:

Non-stick rolling pin

Small palette knife

Dresden tool

Dogbone/ball tool

Heart cutter, 2.5cm (1in)

Small sieve

Instructions:

1 Cut a small pea-sized piece of dark chocolate modelling paste into four to make legs. Roll each to form 0.5cm (¼in) oval shapes.

2 Use the non-stick rolling pin to roll out the white chocolate modelling paste thinly. Cut out the heart shape. Cut into three sections as shown.

3 Shape the rest of the dark chocolate modelling paste to a pointed oval. Pinch to form a small tail at the rounded end. Stroke and smooth the sides and top of the head end to square off the shape.

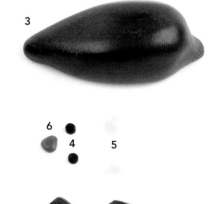

4 Press the sections of white on to form the characteristic stripes on the head. Mark eye sockets using a Dresden tool. Insert the black eyes.

5 Make two very small balls of white chocolate modelling paste for the ears. Lay them in position and push them in with the small end of the dogbone/ball tool, supporting the back of the ear with your finger to help to cup it.

6 Shape a tiny piece of pale chocolate modelling paste into a triangle. Attach to form the nose. Mark nostrils with the Dresden tool.

7 Attach the legs under the body.

8 Squeeze a little piping gel into the eyes to make them look rounded and shiny.

9 Use a small sieve to lightly sprinkle icing sugar over the back, making sure you do not get any on the head by protecting it with your hand.

Poodle

Materials:

30g (1oz) dark chocolate modelling paste

Edible black eyes (see page 6)

Piping gel

Tools:

Non-stick rolling pin

Cutting wheel

Small palette knife

Dresden tool

Texturing sponge

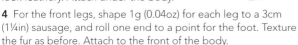

Instructions:

1 To make strands of fur, use the non-stick rolling pin to roll out dark chocolate modelling paste thinly to a strip approximately 1 x 5cm (³/₈ x 2in). Use a cutting wheel or knife to cut very narrow triangles.

2 Shape 10g (¹/₃oz) of dark chocolate modelling paste to a 3cm (1¼in) cone for the body. Mark fur with the texturing sponge or a cocktail stick.

3 Make a thin 2cm (¾in) carrot for the tail. Mark fur with the texturing sponge. Snip little cuts into the sides of the tail to make it look feathery. Attach under the body.

4 For the front legs, shape 1g (0.04oz) for each leg to a 3cm (1¼in) sausage, and roll one end to a point for the foot. Texture the fur as before. Attach to the front of the body.

5 For the back legs, shape 1g (0.04oz) for each leg to a 2cm (¾in) cone. Texture the fur as before. Attach to the bottom of the body.

6 Form a pear shape from 5g (¹/₆oz) of paste by rolling one end of a ball between your fingers. Turn the narrow end up slightly. Indent with the Dresden tool for the eyes. Insert black eyes. Shape two tiny sausages of paste and attach to form eyebrows. Mark the mouth with a knife. Make a hole where the nose will go.

7 Make two very small peas of paste into 1cm (³/₈in) triangles for the ears. Texture as before. Attach each one to the head with one point of the triangle.

8 Stick the head to the top of the body.

9 Attach strands of fur around the nose hole, hanging down each side of the nose. Press them on with the Dresden tool, adding more strands to tidy the joins. Tweak the tips of the fur gently to look curly. Repeat, adding fur to the top of the head.

10 Make a tiny ball of paste for the nose. Press it into place and mark nostrils with the Dresden tool.

11 Squeeze a little piping gel into the eyes to make them look rounded and shiny.

Mole

Materials:

10g (⅓oz) dark chocolate modelling paste

Edible black eyes (see page 6)

5g (⅙oz) pale chocolate modelling paste (see Mouse, page 8)

Piping gel

Tools:

Small palette knife

Dresden tool

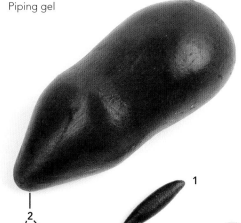

1

2

3

4

Instructions:

1 Shape a very small sausage of dark chocolate modelling paste for the tail.

2 Shape the rest of the dark chocolate modelling paste to a 4cm (1½in) pointed oval for the body. Roll it between your fingers to form the neck. Indent with the Dresden tool for the eyes. Insert black eyes. Attach the tail.

3 Attach a tiny ball of pale chocolate modelling paste for the nose.

4 For the front feet, shape two very small pea-sized pieces of pale chocolate modelling paste each to 1cm (⅜in) ovals. Flatten slightly and mark long toes with the Dresden tool. Attach the front feet to the body at the neck.

5 Back feet. Make in the same way as the front feet, but smaller. Attach to the body.

6 Squeeze a little piping gel into the eyes to make them look rounded and shiny.

24

Guinea Pig

Materials:

10g (1/3oz) white chocolate modelling paste

Edible black eyes (see page 6)

5g (1/6oz) dark chocolate modelling paste

Tiny piece pale chocolate modelling paste (see Mouse, page 8)

Piping gel

Tools:

Small palette knife

Dresden tool

Small non-stick rolling pin

Heart cutter, 1.25cm (1/2in)

Dogbone/ball tool

Instructions:

1 Shape a 3.5cm (1 3/8in) pointed oval from the white chocolate modelling paste. Gently pinch the head. Make the mouth with the end of the knife. Make a tiny triangle nose from pale chocolate modelling paste and press it on.

2 Use the non-stick rolling pin to roll out the dark chocolate modelling paste thinly. Cut out two hearts with the heart cutter. Press them on with the points facing towards the nose. Indent for the eyes using the Dresden tool. Insert the black eyes.

3 Make small carrot shapes of different sizes up to 1cm (3/8in) long from the dark chocolate modelling paste. Press into place at the tail end with the points all facing forward. Mark with the Dresden tool to blend in the pieces and make them look look like hair.

4 Make two tiny balls of pale chocolate modelling paste for the ears. Lay them in position and push them in with the small end of the dogbone/ball tool, supporting the back of the ear with your finger to help to cup it to a rounded shape.

5 Squeeze a little piping gel into the eyes to make them look rounded and shiny.

Giraffe

Materials:

25g (just under 1oz) white chocolate modelling paste

10g ($^1/_3$oz) milk chocolate modelling paste

Edible black eyes (see page 6)

Piping gel

Tools:

Non-stick rolling pin

Small palette knife

Cutting wheel

Dresden tool

Small sharp pointed scissors

Smile tool/drinking straw

Tiny 0.5 cm (¼in) and medium 1cm (³/₈in) heart cutters

Instructions:

1 Use the non-stick rolling pin to roll out the milk chocolate modelling paste thinly. Cut 20–30 of the different sized hearts for the markings.

2 Shape 10g ($^1/_3$oz) of white chocolate modelling paste to a 3cm (1¼in) oval for the body. Roll one end between your fingers to form the neck. Body plus neck should be 5cm (2in) long. Bend the neck up. Make a dip at the top of the neck where the head will go. Press the cut-out hearts all over the body.

3 For the rear legs, make two 2g (0.1oz) balls of white chocolate modelling paste. Roll one end of each ball between your fingers to 3cm (1¼in) long. Pinch the foot end to make it flat. Flatten the rounded end slightly and bend to make a knee. Attach one leg at the back of the body with the knee bending back so that the foot faces forwards. Attach the second leg under the body with the foot in the same direction as the first. Press a small heart on the base of each foot, and all over the legs.

4 For the front legs, make two 1g (0.04oz) balls of white chocolate modelling paste. Roll each to a 3cm (1¼in) sausage. Pinch the foot end to make it flat. Bend to make a knee. Attach both legs at the front of the body with the knees bending so that the feet face back. Press a small heart on the base of each foot, and over the legs.

5 For the tail, roll a small pea-sized piece of white chocolate modelling paste to a 3cm (1¼in) sausage. Press two or three of the hearts in line. Cut a thin tail down the middle. Attach to the body.

6 For the horns, make two 0.5cm (¼in) golf tee shapes from milk chocolate modelling paste.

7 For the ears, cut a very small ball of the white modelling paste in half. Pinch at each end to make points. Flatten slightly and press in the centre with a Dresden tool to hollow each ear. Attach to the head.

8 For the head, shape 3.5g (0.12oz) of white chocolate modelling paste to a 2cm (¾in) pointed pear shape. Cut the mouth with scissors and curve the bottom lip down. Make indentations for the eyes, ears and horns using the Dresden tool. Insert black eyes. Attach two tiny milk chocolate modelling paste sausages for the eyebrows. Press one of the hearts on for the nose and others over the head. Mark the nostrils with the Dresden tool.

9 Attach the head on top of the neck. Stick the ears in place on the back of the head. Push the narrow end of the horns into the holes in the top of the head.

10 Squeeze a little piping gel into the eyes to make them look rounded and shiny.

Porcupine

Materials:

10g (1/3oz) dark chocolate
  modelling paste

5g (1/6oz) white chocolate
  modelling paste

Cocoa powder mixed with
  alcohol or lemon essence
  for painting

Icing sugar

Piping gel

Tools:

Non-stick rolling pin

Small palette knife

Cutting wheel

Dresden tool

Paintbrush/waterbrush filled
  with alcohol or lemon
  essence for painting

Small sharp pointed scissors

Small sieve

Instructions:

1 To make the spines. Use the non-stick rolling pin to roll out the white chocolate modelling paste thinly to a strip approximately 2 x 8cm (¾ x 3⅛in). Paint thin cocoa stripes along the length of the strip. Use a cutting wheel or knife to cut very narrow triangles to make the spines.

2 For the legs, cut a 1g (0.04oz) ball of dark chocolate modelling paste into four. Roll each to form a 1cm (⅜in) carrot. Bend each leg to form a foot. Stick them together in pairs. Stand them upright.

3 Shape the dark chocolate modelling paste to a 5cm (2in) cone for the body. Mark ears and eyes with the Dresden tool. Mark a 'v' shape for the nose with small sharp pointed scissors.

4 Attach the spines to the body by smoothing them in with the Dresden tool, starting at the back and working forward to the head. Paint with the cocoa mix over the tips and base of the spines.

5 Attach the legs under the body.

6 Sprinkle the spines with icing sugar using the small sieve.

7 Squeeze a little piping gel into the eyes to make them look rounded and shiny.

30

Armadillo

Materials:

10g (1/3oz) dark chocolate modelling paste

10g (1/3oz) white chocolate modelling paste

Tools:

Non-stick rolling pin

Small palette knife

Dresden tool

5cm (2in) oval cutter

Texturing sponge or cocktail stick

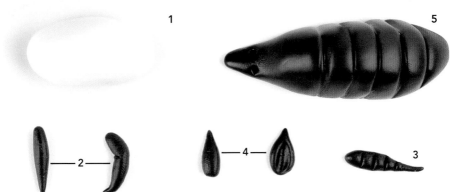

Instructions:

1 As the armadillo model has very thin legs, the weight of the body would make the legs collapse, so make a little base to stand the body on. Use the non-stick rolling pin to roll out the white chocolate modelling paste. Cut out the oval shape using the oval cutter. Roll 5g (1/6oz) of white chocolate modelling paste to a 3cm (1¼in) sausage. Press into place on top of the flat oval.

2 Cut a small pea-sized piece of dark chocolate modelling paste into four to make the legs. Roll each to form small 1cm (3/8in) carrot shapes. Bend to form a knee and a pointed foot. Press to attach them to the sides of the base.

3 Make another tiny carrot shape for the tail. Mark lines across it with the palette knife. Attach it to the base.

4 Cut a very small ball of the dark chocolate paste in half. Pinch at each end to make points. Flatten slightly and press in the centre with a Dresden tool to hollow each ear.

5 Use the rest of the dark chocolate modelling paste to make a 5cm (2in) oval. Roll between your fingers to form one end to a narrow point, the other end to a shorter point. Place down on a work surface. Gently stroke the sides to bring the edges flat down to the surface. Mark lines across the back for the hard skin, using the palette knife. Texture the surface by pressing with a texturing sponge or by marking with a cocktail stick.

6 Attach the ears by pushing them in with a Dresden tool.

7 Mark the eyes with a Dresden tool. The eyes are very small, so I have not used black inserts, but they could be finished with a little piping gel if desired.

8 Use the palette knife to release the body from the surface. Lift it on to the base and press gently to attach. Any fingerprints can be smoothed out by stroking gently with your fingers.

Goat

Materials:

25g (just under 1oz) dark chocolate modelling paste

10g (1/3oz) white chocolate modelling paste

10g (1/3oz) milk chocolate modelling paste

Edible black eyes (see page 6)

Piping gel

Tools:

Non-stick rolling pin

Small palette knife

Cutting wheel

Dresden tool

Small sharp pointed scissors

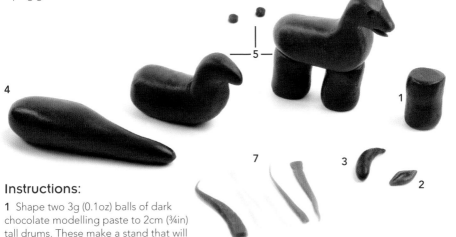

Instructions:

1 Shape two 3g (0.1oz) balls of dark chocolate modelling paste to 2cm (¾in) tall drums. These make a stand that will not be seen.

2 Cut a very small ball of the paste in half to make the ears. Pinch at each end to make points. Flatten slightly and press in the centre with a Dresden tool to hollow each ear.

3 For the horns, make two small curved carrot shapes from dark chocolate modelling paste.

4 For the body, shape 10g (1/3oz) of dark chocolate modelling paste to a 4cm (1½in) oval. Roll one end between your fingers to narrow it. The total length should now be about 6cm (2³/8in).

5 Bend the narrow end up for the neck then bend the tip forwards to make the head. Snip the mouth with sharp pointed scissors. Make indentations with the Dresden tool for the eyes, ears and horns. Insert black eyes. Attach the body to the top of the stand, making sure it is balanced.

6 Attach the ears and horns to the head.

7 Use the non-stick rolling pin to roll out the white and milk chocolate modelling paste thinly to strips approximately 3 x 8cm (1¼ x 3¹/8in). Use a cutting wheel or knife to cut very narrow triangles to make the hair for the body and the tail. Making slightly different lengths will look more natural. Cut a few shorter, finer strands for the fringe.

8 Attach the hair all over the body from the centre of the back using the different shades of chocolate modelling paste. Hide the stand completely with the hair. Make a fringe coming over from the top of the head.

9 Squeeze a little piping gel into the eyes to make them look rounded and shiny.

Sleeping Bear

Materials:

40g (1⅓oz)
  dark chocolate modelling
  paste

1g (0.04oz) milk chocolate
  modelling paste

5g (⅙oz) white chocolate
  modelling paste

Tools:

Small palette knife

Non-stick rolling pin

Dresden tool

Dogbone/ball tool

Heart cutter, 2cm (¾in)

Smile tool/drinking straw

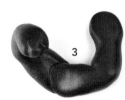

Instructions:

1 Shape four 5g (⅙oz) sausages of dark chocolate modelling paste to 4cm (1½in) for the legs and arms. Roll between fingers to form knees/elbows and ankles/wrists. For the legs, bend the foot and pinch gently to shape a heel. Mark fingers/toes on hands and feet with a Dresden tool.

2 Lay one leg on the surface, bent outwards. Lay the other leg with the foot resting on the first leg. Press the top end of the legs together, flattening slightly.

3 Lay the arms on the surface. Press them together at the shoulder end.

4 Shape 10g (⅓oz) of dark chocolate modelling paste to an oval to make the tummy. Use the non-stick rolling pin to roll out the white chocolate modelling paste thinly. Cut out the heart shape. Smooth on to the tummy.

5 Attach the arms and legs under the body.

6 Make two very small balls of dark chocolate modelling paste for the ears. Save a tiny piece of the dark paste to make a ball for the nose. Shape the rest of the paste to a ball for the head. Lay the ears in position and push them in with the small end of the dogbone/ball tool, supporting the back of the ear with your finger to help to cup it.

7 Mark sleeping eyes by pressing in the smile tool/drinking straw.

8 Shape the milk chocolate modelling paste to a 1cm (⅜in) oval for the muzzle. Attach under the closed eyes. Mark a hole for the nose. Attach the nose.

9 Mark the mouth with the smile tool/drinking straw, as shown.

10 Attach the head to the body. Position the arms and legs as desired.

Otter

Materials:

15g (½oz) milk chocolate modelling paste

2g (0.1oz) pale chocolate modelling paste (see Mouse, page 8)

Edible black eyes (see page 6)

Tiny piece of dark chocolate modelling paste for nose

Piping gel

Tools:

Small palette knife

Dresden tool

Non-stick rolling pin

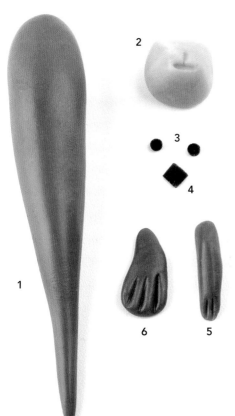

Instructions:

1 Shape 10g (⅓oz) of milk chocolate modelling paste to a carrot 8cm (3⅛in) long. Press in the wide end where the head will go.

2 For the head, shape the pale chocolate modelling paste into a ball and flatten the top and sides of the face to make it more angular. Mark an upside down 'T' for the mouth with a knife. Indent the eyes, ears and nose with the Dresden tool. Attach the head to the body.

3 Insert black eyes. Mark dots for the whiskers.

4 For the nose, use the non-stick rolling pin to roll out the dark chocolate modelling paste thinly. Cut out a tiny square with the small palette knife. Stick on the nose and mark nostrils with the Dresden tool.

5 For the front legs, shape two 0.5g (0.02oz) pieces of paste into sausages. Mark toes with the knife. Attach to the body just below the head.

6 For the back feet, form two 0.5g (0.02oz) pieces of paste each to a 1.5cm (⅝in) carrot. Flatten slightly and mark feet with the Dresden tool. Attach to the body as shown.

7 Squeeze a little piping gel into the eyes to make them look rounded and shiny.

39

Leopard Gecko

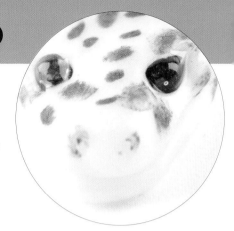

Materials:

10g (⅓oz) white chocolate modelling paste

Edible black eyes (see page 6)

Cocoa powder mixed with alcohol or lemon essence for painting

Piping gel

Tools:

Small palette knife

Dresden tool

Paintbrush/waterbrush for painting

Instructions:

1 For the legs, cut a large pea-sized ball (2g/0.1oz) of white chocolate modelling paste into four. Roll each to a 2.5cm (1in) carrot. Press with the Dresden tool to form toes at the pointed end of each leg.

2 For the body, roll the rest of the paste to a 9cm (3½in) carrot. Roll between your fingers to form a neck approximately 2cm (¾in) from the wide end, and then roll 4cm (1½in) from the narrow end for the tail.

3 Shape the head by stroking and gently pinching to flatten it. Mark a wide mouth with the small palette knife. Mark nostrils and eyes with the Dresden tool. Insert black eyes and push them in with the Dresden tool.

4 Gently pinch along the length of the tail to form a ridge. Curve the body and tail to look natural.

5 Attach the two legs at the same time with toes pointing upwards, and then bend each leg to form a knee and foot pointing forwards.

6 Paint cocoa spots all over the gecko.

7 Squeeze a little piping gel into the eyes to make them look rounded and shiny.

Pony

Materials:

25g (just under 1oz) milk chocolate modelling paste

10g (1/3oz) white chocolate modelling paste

Edible black eyes (see page 6)

Piping gel

Tools:

Non-stick rolling pin

Small palette knife

Cutting wheel

Dresden tool

Small sharp pointed scissors

Smile tool/drinking straw

Heart cutter, 0.5cm (1/4in)

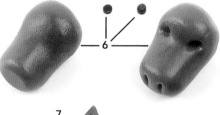

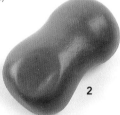

Instructions:

1 To make the hair, use the non-stick rolling pin to roll out the white chocolate modelling paste thinly to a strip 2 x 8cm (3/4 x 3 1/8in). Use a cutting wheel or knife to cut very narrow triangles to make the hair for the mane and the tail. Cut one heart for the marking on the head.

2 To make the body, shape 10g (1/3oz) of milk chocolate modelling paste to a 3cm (1 1/4in) oval. Roll it between your fingers to form a waist. Make a dip on the top of one end where the head will go.

3 Make two 3g (0.1oz) balls of milk chocolate modelling paste for the rear legs. Roll one end between your fingers to 3cm (1 1/4in). Flatten the rounded end and roll it towards the narrow end.

4 Make two 3cm (1 1/4in) sausages of milk chocolate modelling paste for the front legs. Roll each leg between your fingers to form knees.

5 For the hooves, shape 2g (0.1oz) of white chocolate modelling paste to a sausage with flat ends. Cut into four even slices. Pinch gently to keep the small drum shape. Attach to the end of the legs and smooth in the joins. Mark horseshoes on the back hooves with the smile tool/drinking straw. Attach the legs to the body.

6 For the head, roll a 5g (¹/₆oz) ball of milk chocolate modelling paste between your fingers at one end to make a fat pear shape. Mark nostrils and eyes with the Dresden tool. Insert black eyes. Make the mouth with the smile tool/drinking straw. Attach the tiny white heart.

7 Cut a very small ball of the milk chocolate modelling paste in half for the ears. Pinch at each end to make points. Flatten slightly and press in the centre with a Dresden tool to hollow each ear. Attach to the head.

8 Attach the head to the body.

9 Attach the strands of hair for the tail and mane, pressing the ends firmly with the Dresden tool.

10 Squeeze a little piping gel into the eyes to make them look rounded and shiny.

Reindeer

Materials:

35g (1¼oz)
milk chocolate modelling
paste

5g (⅙oz) dark chocolate
modelling paste

5g (⅙oz) white chocolate
modelling paste

Edible black eyes (see page 6)

Piping gel

Icing sugar

Tools:

Non-stick rolling pin

Small sharp pointed
scissors

Cutting wheel

Small palette knife

Dresden tool

Heart cutters, 2cm (¾in)
and 0.5cm (¼in)

Small sieve

Instructions:

1 Make a small pea-size piece of dark chocolate modelling paste. Cut it in half and roll each to a 3cm (1¼in) pointed sausage. Cut into each pointed end with a cutting wheel or knife. Fold slightly off-centre and roll the fold between your fingers. Open up the cut points to look like simple antlers.

2 For the legs, shape 10g (⅓oz) of milk chocolate modelling paste to a 3cm (1¼in) long drum. Square off the edges by pinching and stroking to form a rectangular box. Mark down the length of each face of the box with a palette knife to give the appearance of four long, straight legs. Make sure the top and bottom are flat.

3 Use the non-stick rolling pin to roll out the dark chocolate modelling paste thinly. Cut out two of the smaller heart shapes. Press the little hearts on one end of the leg block to look like feet. Leave the leg block to cool lying down before standing it up for the final assembly.

4 Roll out the white chocolate modelling paste thinly. Cut out the larger heart shape.

5 Shape 20g (⅔oz) of milk chocolate modelling paste to a 4cm (1½in) oval for the body. Make a dip on top of one end for the head. Snip with sharp pointed scissors to form a tail. Press the cut-out white chocolate heart on to the front of the body for the chest.

6 Cut a very small ball of the paste in half for the ears. Pinch at each end to make points. Flatten slightly and press in the centre with a Dresden tool to hollow each ear.

7 Shape the head by rolling one end of a 5g (⅙oz) ball of milk chocolate modelling paste to form a pear shape. Mark the eyes with the Dresden tool. Insert black eyes. Make two holes for the antlers. Mark the mouth with a knife.

8 Make a tiny triangle of dark chocolate modelling paste for the nose. Press the nose into place. Attach the ears.

9 Attach the head to the top of the body.

10 Attach the body to the top of the legs, making sure it balances properly. Press to make sure it sticks. Any fingerprints can be smoothed out by polishing with your fingers.

11 Press the antlers into place.

12 Squeeze a little piping gel into the eyes to make them look rounded and shiny.

13 Use a small sieve to lightly sprinkle icing sugar over the back and head.

Prairie Dog

Materials:

20g (²/₃oz) white chocolate modelling paste

Edible black eyes (see page 6)

Tiny piece of pale chocolate modelling paste (see Mouse, page 8)

Tiny piece of milk chocolate modelling paste

Cocoa powder

Piping gel

Tools:

Small palette knife

Non-stick rolling pin

Dresden tool

Cocktail stick

Small sieve

Instructions:

1 For the body, shape 10g (¹/₃oz) of white chocolate modelling paste to a 4cm (1½in) oval. Roll it between your fingers to form a neck. Pinch the head forward to a point for the nose.

2 Indent for the eyes and ears using the Dresden tool. Insert black eyes.

3 For the nose, attach a tiny milk chocolate modelling paste triangle. Mark the nostrils with the Dresden tool.

4 Use the non-stick rolling pin to roll a tiny piece of pale chocolate modelling paste thinly. Cut a tiny rectangle and mark a line down the centre to make the teeth. Attach them under the nose.

5 For the back legs, shape two 1g (0.04oz) balls of paste to 3cm (1¼in) cones. Flatten the rounded end slightly and roll towards the foot. Mark toes with a knife. Attach to the body, pressing both on at the same time.

6 For the front legs, roll two 0.5g (0.02oz) balls of paste to 1cm (³/₈in) carrot shapes. Mark toes with a knife. Attach to the body, pressing both on at the same time. Position the back legs in the same way.

7 Shape a very small sausage of white chocolate paste, and attach it for the tail.

8 Push a cocktail stick up through the base to hold the prairie dog while you sprinkle cocoa powder with a sieve over the back, sides and head, leaving the tummy pale.

9 Squeeze a little piping gel into the eyes to make them look rounded and shiny.

10 Remove the cocktail stick carefully without smudging the cocoa powder.

Acknowledgements

My thanks to the lovely team at Search Press, especially Sophie Kersey, Marrianne Mercer and Debbie Patterson. Special thanks to Ruby and Jack for the idea of making their pets – a guinea pig and a leopard gecko. Also thanks to my sister Annie for the idea of making Basil, her toy poodle.

Publisher's Note

If you would like more information about sugarcraft, try the following books by the same author, all published by Search Press:
Twenty to Make Sugar Animals
Twenty to Make Sugar Birds
Twenty to Make Sugar Fairies
Sensational Sugar Animals

You are invited to visit the author's website:
www.franklysweet.co.uk